Bipolar Disorder

The complete guide to understanding, dealing with, managing, and improving bipolar disorder, including treatment options and bipolar disorder remedies!

Copyright 2015

Table of Contents

Introduction 1
Chapter 1: Understanding Bipolar Disorder 2
Chapter 2: Symptoms of Bipolar Disorder 9
Chapter 3: Bipolar Medications 14
Chapter 4: Psychotherapy and Alternative Treatments for Bipolar Patients 21
Chapter 5: Lifestyle Changes 24
Chapter 6: Other Tips for Coping with Bipolar Disorder 29
Conclusion 36

Introduction

I want to thank you and congratulate you for downloading the book, "Bipolar Disorder".

This book contains helpful information about this mental illness, what it is, and how to manage and improve it.

You will soon learn about the different types of Bipolar disorder, the signs and symptoms of each type, and how to determine if you or a loved one is suffering from this condition.

This book explains the different medical treatment options, including the different medications that you may be prescribed, along with several different forms of therapy.

You will also be provided with some self-help solutions that will assist you in managing and improving your condition. This includes tips to help you stay organized, punctual, grounded, and not over-impulsive during both manic and depressive episodes.

This book will provide you with some useful tips and techniques that will allow you to begin successfully managing and improving your condition!

Thanks again for downloading this book, I hope you enjoy it!

Chapter 1:
Understanding Bipolar Disorder

Bipolar disorder is one of the most common mental diseases today. More than 5 million people in the United States have this mental illness, according to the National Institute of Mental Health. Many famous people also have this condition. In fact, these celebrities are all diagnosed with this mental illness:

- Mel Gibson
- Vivien Leigh
- Carrie Fisher
- Jean-Claude Van Damme
- Nicki Minaj
- Demi Lovato
- Catherine Zeta-Jones
- Sinead Connor
- Ben Stiller
- Ashley Judd
- Linda Hamilton
- Russell Brand

Bipolar disorder is a mental disease that has alternating periods of depression and elation. It is also known as manic depression or manic depressive disorder.

People with this disorder have extreme and rapid changes in mood from depression to euphoria.

Manic episodes of this mental condition are often characterized by extreme euphoria. Bipolar patients who have a manic episode may be talkative, energetic, and restless. These patients feel powerful and they often overestimate their capabilities. They go on spending sprees or partake in impulsive sexual behavior. Many experts say that manic episodes can be productive. Artists who have this illness are very creative when they are in a manic state. Demi Lovato said that she can write up to seven songs in a night during her manic episodes.

Bipolar patients often experience the following symptoms of depressive episodes like crying, sadness, loss of energy, sense of worthlessness, sleep problems, and loss of pleasure. Depressive episodes of bipolar patients can be dangerous. They can lead to unemployment, isolation, and even death.

Because the patterns of lows and highs vary for each patient, this disorder is difficult to diagnose. For some patients, manic and depressive episodes could last for weeks or months. Because of this, experts have divided the disorder into several types.

Types of Bipolar Disorder

1. **Bipolar I**

Bipolar I is the most severe type of the disorder. A Bipolar I diagnosis necessitates at least 1 manic episode in the patient's lifetime with a duration of 7 days or more. The manic episode must impair a person's professional or personal life.

Manic Bipolar I patients often experience mood instability, elation, and irritability. At least three of the following symptoms must be present before a doctor can give a diagnosis:

- Less need for sleep
- Grandiosity
- Pressured speech
- Excessive talking
- Inability to concentrate
- Excessive engagement in pleasurable activities such as sex and use of drugs.

People with Bipolar I also have occasional extreme depressive episodes which have the following signs and symptoms:

- Fatigue
- Insomnia
- Weight loss or weight gain
- Low self-esteem
- Thoughts of death and suicide

People with Bipolar I may also have mixed episodes. This means that patients with Bipolar I may be happy and sad at the same time. This happens when patients have rapid mood fluctuations. They are happy for an hour and then they are sad for another hour.

2. Bipolar II

Bipolar II is a milder form of the disorder. It is similar to Bipolar I because Bipolar II patients also experience mood swings. But, the manic episodes of Bipolar II patients are less intense. Doctors call these episodes "hypomania".

During hypomanic episodes, patients will experience the following:

- Increased energy

- Loud and rapid speech

- Flying from one idea to the next

Patients who have hypomanic episodes are pleasant and fun to be around. They are often considered as the "life of the party". They make jokes and they have an infectious positive mood.

While hypomanic episodes have positive effects on the patient's personality, they can also lead to unhealthy and erratic behavior. In fact, hypomanic episodes can develop into full-blown manic episodes that could affect the patient's ability to carry out their day to day tasks.

3. Rapid Cycling

Rapid Cycling is characterized by a pattern of frequent manic, hypomanic, and depressive episodes. Patients with rapid cycling bipolar disorder often have 4 or more episodes of depression or mania in a year. These episodes can occur any point and can come and go over the years.

4. Cyclothymia

Cyclothymia is the mildest form of this disorder. It has less severe depressive episodes and several hypomanic episodes. These episodes can alternate for about two years.

Causes of Bipolar Disorder

The exact cause of this mental disorder is still unknown. But, many experts and psychologists believe that a lot of factors can contribute to bipolar disorder, including:

1. Chemical Imbalance

Many experts believe that the disorder is caused by a chemical imbalance in the brain. Brain chemicals or neurotransmitters such as dopamine, serotonin, neurotransmitters, and noradrenaline control most brain functions.

Several studies show that manic episodes occur when noraderanaline levels are too high. Depressive episodes happen when the noradrenaline levels are too low.

2. Genetics

Many studies show that genetics play an important role in the development of this disease. It can run in the family.

But, there is no single gene that can cause this mental disorder. A combination of environmental and genetic factors can cause this disease.

3. Hormonal Problems

Studies show that hormonal imbalance, especially during pregnancy, is one of the causes of manic depression.

4. Environmental Triggers

There are many environmental factors that trigger manic depression including:

- Stress – Too much stress can trigger bipolar symptoms.
- Divorce or Breakup – People with relationship issues are more susceptible to developing manic-depressive illness.
- Physical, Sexual, and Emotional Abuse
- Death of a loved one or a family member

5. Physical illness

Physical sickness is not the cause of this disease. But, it can cause some symptoms of manic depression. Some medications can cause the symptoms of depression and hypomania.

6. Weather

Seasonal factors can play an important role in the development of this disorder. The rapid increase of sunshine can actually cause both depression and mania.

Difference between Ordinary Mood Swings and Bipolar Disorder

There is a difference between ordinary mood swings and bipolar disorder. Bipolar mood swings are more intense than the ordinary mood swings.

A typical "bad mood" is gone after a few days or even hours. But, the depression and mania that come with this mental illness can last for weeks or even months.

Lastly, ordinary mood swings do not disrupt human cognition and functioning. Bipolar mood swings, on other hand, can severely disrupt your life.

Chapter 2:
Symptoms of Bipolar Disorder

If you are suspecting that you have bipolar disorder, check if you have the following symptoms:

1. Inability to complete projects and tasks.

If you have many pending projects and tasks, you may have a manic-depressive disorder. Bipolar people often plan grand projects. They often start grand and unrealistic projects. They go from task to task never really accomplishing anything because they are easily distracted.

2. Euphoria

The manic episode of people with this disorder is often characterized by euphoria. Bipolar patients often have a heightened sense of accomplishment and level of happiness. They often engage in many grand and goal-oriented activities and projects.

When patients are in a manic state, they feel some kind of "high". They feel happiness and bliss. When bipolar people are in a manic state, they often have high energy. They feel like they can accomplish anything.

3. Racing Thoughts

Bipolar people often have racing thoughts. They often over analyze things and they have difficulty focusing on one thing. Their speech and thoughts often jump from one random unrelated topic to another. This increases their distractibility. This symptom can hold these people back from accomplishing something really important and finishing their goal oriented tasks.

During extreme manic periods, people who suffer from this mental disease have a hard time curtailing their thoughts. But, during a milder episode called "hypomania", bipolar patients can curtail and control these racing thoughts.

4. Rapid Speech

Bipolar patients often speak rapidly. This is one of the manic symptoms of this mental illness. They have a hard time following a logical train of thought. They often just jump from one topic to another. They often feel restless and they often overestimate their own talents and abilities.

5. Increase Physical Activity

When bipolar people are experiencing a manic episode, they will have extreme levels of energy. To help release this energy, they often turn to physical activity like rigid exercise. If you suddenly feel the need to exercise excessively to use energy, it could be a strong indication that you have this mental disease.

People with this disorder often engage in impulsive sexual activities to release their energy. During a manic episode, a bipolar patient may engage in excessive and risky sexual behavior and sexual activities without considering the possible negative consequences of these behaviors. This behavior can lead to a lot of problems like sexually transmitted disease and unwanted pregnancy.

6. Irritation

Bipolar people get irritated easily, even by the most trivial things. Agitation and irritation are common in both depressive and manic episodes of bipolar patients.

7. Drug or Alcohol Abuse

Bipolar patients often turn to alcohol and drugs. What's worse is that the use of alcohol and drugs can further increase the mood instability caused by this disease.

8. Insomnia

During a manic state, patients often have large bursts of euphoria and energy. This makes it difficult for them to sleep because they will not feel exhausted or tired. They often use their excessive energy rather than sleep.

9. Missing work days

Bipolar people often have a hard time following a schedule. Because of this, they often miss school, work, and other commitments. They miss work because they often feel overwhelmed by the task at hand. They also skip work because they think that they have other more important things to do. When patients are in a depressive state, they would rather sleep and watch TV than get up and work.

10. Depression

Bipolar people are often depressed after a euphoric and manic state. When they have depression, they have extremely low energy and they have problems with appetite. They also have a problem focusing on one thing.

They often stay home for a couple of days. In some extreme cases, these patients can stay at home for weeks, even months. They feel hopeless and helpless. They have appetite changes and they are often angry and irritable. They often isolate themselves from their friends. They also lack confidence. They can be indecisive, sad, miserable, unhappy, and guilty. They feel tired all the time and they have headaches and muscle pains.

11. Fatigue

People with manic depression often feel tired all the time. They also have frequent headaches and muscle pains. During depressive episodes, they often go to bed early and they stay in bed until late afternoon. They tend to lack motivation to do important things like spending time with loved ones or work.

They often feel mentally bogged down despite of the fact that they have slept for more than ten hours. They also have a lack of desire and interest in the things that use to interest them.

12. Chronic Pain

Patients with this disorder often experience chronic pain for no reason or known cause. This happens during their depressive episode.

13. Hallucinations and delusions

Patients often have delusions and hallucinations during their manic episodes. They often have delusions of grandeur. In some extreme cases, patients have wild thoughts, such as that they want to be the President of the United States.

14. Impulsiveness and impaired judgment

People who have this disorder are often impulsive. They do things without thinking about the consequences. They often shop excessively. As a result, they have maxed out credit cards. They often choose lovers and friends that are bad for them.

15. Thoughts of death and suicide

When patients have depressive episodes, they often have thoughts of death. They imagine that they are dying or that they have a terminal disease. Depressed patients also have recurring thoughts of suicide. Studies show that bipolar people may attempt to commit suicide. In fact, many of them are living as if they have a "death wish".

These symptoms can often keep bipolar patients from living a happy, fulfilling, and successful life. These symptoms can keep them isolated and feeling misunderstood.

Chapter 3:
Bipolar Medications

Bipolar treatment is the combination of drugs and therapy. If you suspect, that you have a bipolar disorder, go to a psychiatrist right away. This mental disorder often requires lifelong treatment. You need to see your therapist regularly even if you are feeling better.

Treatment is usually done by a psychiatrist. But, there may also be a team of psychiatric nurses, social workers, and psychologists who may help you during your treatment. Below are some of the common treatment methods:

1. Hospitalization

Your doctor may recommend hospitalization if you are behaving dangerously or if you are suicidal.

2. Initial Treatment

Your physician will give you medicines to balance your moods and behavior right away. Once the symptoms are under control, you will work with your psychiatrist to find the best combination of long term treatment.

3. Continued Treatment

Patients need maintenance treatment to manage their illness. Skipping medications may lead to a relapse of symptoms.

4. **Substance Abuse Treatment**

Patients often turn to alcohol and drugs. So, it may be necessary to undergo substance abuse treatment. Confinement in a rehabilitation facility may be necessary in some cases.

There are also number of medications used to treat this disease, including:

- **Antidepressants**

Your doctor may ask you to take antidepressants like:

- Zoloft (Setraline)
- Celexa (Citalopram)
- Luvox (Flouzamine)
- Paxil (Paroxetine)
- Lexapro (Escitalopram)
- Emsam (Selegiline)
- Nardil (Phenelzine)
- Parnate (Isocarboxazid)
- Pamelor (Nortrityline)
- Nopramin (Desipramine)
- Tofranil (Imipramine)

But, antidepressants have many side effects including:

- Nervousness
- Nausea
- Rash
- Diarrhea
- Agitation
- Loss of libido
- Insomnia
- Weight loss
- Weight gain
- Dry mouth
- Muscle Twitching

- **Lithium**

Lithium is an effective mood stabilizer. It prevents highs and lows. Patients can use lithium for years. But, lithium may cause kidney and thyroid problems. It can also cause dry mouth and certain digestive issues.

- **Anticonvulsants**

Anticonvulsants like divalproex, valproic acid, and lamotrigine are helpful in stabilizing moods. Common side effects of these medications include drowsiness, dizziness, weight gain, liver problems, skin rashes, and blood disorders.

- **Benzodiazepines**

These anti-anxiety drugs may reduce worrying and improve sleep. Your doctor may ask you to take these benzodiazepines:

- Xanax (Alprazolam)
- Klonopin (Clonazepam)
- Ativan (Lorazepam)
- Valium (Diazepam)

But, it is important to note that benzodiazepines have the following side effects:

- Slurred speech
- Laziness
- Drowsiness
- Memory Loss
- Muscle Weakness
- Fatigue
- Lightheadedness

- **Antipsychotics**

These antipsychotic drugs may help ease bipolar symptoms:

- Clorazil (Clozapine)
- Abilify (Aripiprazole)
- Latuda (Lurasidone)
- Geodon (Ziprasidone)
- Saphris (Asenapine)
- Risperdal (Risperidone)
- Zyprexa (Olanzapine)
- Seroquel (Quetiapin

These medicines may have side effects like blurred vision, weight gain, tremors, and sleepiness.

- **Symbyax**

This medication is a combination of flouxitine and olanzapine. It works as a mood stabilizer and an antidepressant. This has the approval of The Food and Drug Authority specifically for the treatment of various types of manic-depressive illness.

- **Calcium Channel Blockers**

Calcium channel blockers are typically used to treat heart diseases and high blood pressure. But, many mental health professionals use these calcium channel blockers to treat manic episodes:

- Verapamil
- Isradipine
- Diltiazem
- Nimodipine

But, it is important to note that calcium channel blockers have side effects, including:

- Weakness
- Leg Swelling
- Irregular Heart Greeting
- Slowed Heart Rate
- Constipation
- Decreased blood pressure

Finding the right medication may be a long trial and error process. It requires patience because most medications need weeks and even months to take full effect.

It is important to note that most medication used for this mental illness can result in birth defects. You have to discuss pregnancy and birth control usage with your doctor.

Chapter 4:
Psychotherapy and Alternative Treatments for Bipolar Patients

There are a lot of things that you need to do to cope with this mental illness. Here are some of the key recovery concepts that you have to adopt to help deal with this illness:

1. You have to be hopeful.

No matter how hard it is, it is possible to experience wellness for a long period of time. You have to believe that things can get better.

2. You have to take responsibility.

You have to take full responsibility in treating your disease. You have to take action to stabilize your moods.

3. You have to educate yourself about the mental condition.

You have to learn as much as you can about your illness. It will be easier for you to cope with this disease if you have ample information about the disease.

4. You have to get support.

You can deal with this mental disorder alone, but it is best to get support from other people, especially from your loved ones.

Psychotherapy is also a very important part of the treatment. These types of therapy may be helpful:

- **Family Therapy**

Family therapy involves seeing a mental health professional with your family members. This type of therapy can help identify and reduce problems and stress within your family. This can also help you and your family members resolve conflicts and problems.

- **Cognitive Behavioral Therapy**

Cognitive behavior therapy is effective in reducing the symptoms of this disease. Cognitive behavioral therapy aims to identify negative and unhealthy beliefs and behaviors.

- **Group Therapy**

This type of therapy allows you to share your struggles and your progress with other bipolar patients. This is best if you want to have a strong support group made of people who understand your struggles.

- **Psychoeducation**

Psychoeducation may help you and your family members understand your mental condition. Psychoeducation can help you get the best treatment and support.

You can also use the following alternative treatments:

1. Omega 3 Fatty Acids

These oils may relieve depression and can help to improve brain function. People who eat a lot of fish have less risk of developing this disease.

2. Magnesium

Several studies show that magnesium may lessen the rapid cycling symptoms of this illness.

3. St. John's Wort

St. John's Wort is a wonder herb is helpful in treating depression. But, it can have diverse effects if you use it with other antidepressants. So, consult your doctor before using this.

4. Massage therapy

Massage therapy can help relieve stress and anxiety which can worsen most bipolar symptoms.

5. Yoga

Studies show that yoga may ease the mood swings and depression associated with this illness.

Chapter 5:
Lifestyle Changes

If you want to improve your condition, you have to make huge changes in your lifestyle, including:

1. **Reach out to other people for support.**

Having a very strong support system is vital to staying healthy and happy. Having someone to have a face to face conversation with can be a huge help in improving your mood and in relieving depression. You do not have to turn to people who can help you. All you need is someone who will listen.

- Turn to your family and friends – You have to open up about your battle to your family and friends. If you are struggling with this mental disease, it's best to live near your family and friends. Loneliness and isolation can cause depression. Regular contact with your loved ones and friends can be therapeutic. Reaching out and asking for support from your loved ones is not a sign of weakness. It will not make you a burden to them. Your family loves you and they would want to help you.

  Ask a friend or a loved one to check in on you every day or every week. You can schedule a weekly date with your partner or your spouse.

- Create new relationships – Loneliness can make the symptoms of this mental disease worse. If you do not have friends or family, create new relationships. Do this by going out more often. You can go to the church. You can volunteer in cause-oriented projects. You can also attend events in your community. You can also meet new people by joining a club.

- Join a support group – There are a lot of support groups that help people with this disease. Spending time with people who can relate to the things that you are going through is very therapeutic.

- Confide in your therapist, counselor, or clergy member.

2. Fight Stress

Stress is one of the powerful triggers of this illness. If you want to improve your condition, you have to keep stress to the minimum. Here are some of the things that you can do to minimize stress in your life:

- Relax – You can use a lot of relaxation techniques to fight stress. You can practice Tai Chi, meditation, or yoga.

- Have fun – Keep your life balanced by doing fun things every now and then. You can go to the beach or read a book. You can also watch funny movies. Play is necessary in maintaining mental stability.

- Listen to music – Music is an instant stress reliever. If you are facing stress, listen to upbeat or relaxing music. Music is food for the soul.

- Stay calm – If you are faced with a stressful situation, do not react right away. Count from one to ten before reacting.

3. Eat healthy foods.

This mental disorder is often caused by a chemical imbalance and nutritional deficiency. Eating healthy foods will help you improve your mood. These foods are:

- Lean meats
- Soy products
- Fresh fruits
- Vegetables
- Low fat dairy
- Nuts
- Seeds

You need to stay away from foods that are rich in trans fats. You need to avoid eating burgers, French fries, and baked goods.

4. Avoid drugs and alcohol

Drugs and alcohol will only worsen your condition. It's best to avoid drugs and alcohol altogether.

5. Exercise.

Exercising will increase your endorphins. Regular moderate exercise will help you stabilize your mood. It will also make you physically healthier and fit.

6. Create a daily routine.

If you want to avoid erratic mood swings, you have to build a daily schedule. You can keep stress at bay by writing a "to do" list. You have to create a certain activity pattern. You have to create a consistent sleep or meal schedule. Wake up and go to bed the same time every day. This will give you a sense of control. This will also help you achieve emotional stability.

7. Avoid caffeine.

Caffeine can alter your mood, so you have to avoid it. Avoid drinking tea, soda, and coffee. Go for fresh juice, instead.

8. Quit smoking.

Nicotine is a mood altering substance. So, it is best to stay away from cigarettes.

9. Get enough sleep.

Aside from having a fixed sleep schedule, you also need to get enough sleep. This is an effective antidote to rapid cycling. See a doctor if you are having sleeping problems.

10. Fight weight gain.

Many medications used to fight manic depression can cause weight gain. Weight gain can worsen depression and self-esteem issues. You have to combat weight gain by exercising and eating low calorie foods.

11. Meditate.

Meditation can help you control mood swings. Meditation can make you feel grounded. It can also help you control your thoughts, your impulses, and your mood.

Find a place that is free of distractions. Turn off all the distractions like your cell phone, computer, and television. Sit in a comfortable position and close your eyes. Take deep breaths. Say "inner peace" as you breathe in and breathe out. Concentrate on your breathing and drop all the other distracting thoughts. Do this for five minutes.

12. Get rid of all the distractions when you are working.

Bipolar people often have a problem with their career because of their inability to focus. To lessen distractibility, you have to eliminate all distractions. Block distracting websites such as Twitter and Facebook when you are working. You can use FocalFilter or StayFocusd to do this.

Check your email only twice a day maximum – once in the morning and once again at 2 p.m. in the afternoon.

Lifestyle changes can help you deal with the symptoms of bipolar disorder. They also can have a lot of other benefits in your life.

Chapter 6:
Other Tips for Coping with Bipolar Disorder

Coping with manic depression can be challenging. But, it is easier if you adopt some of these habits and behaviors:

1. Monitor your mood and symptoms.

If you want to control and stabilize your moods, you have to monitor them. Keep a mood journal and write down how you feel every day. You can also keep a mood chart that would look like this:

Day	**Mood**
Monday	I feel happy ☺ Note: I was so happy so I bought a $1,000 bag. I only have a few dollars left in my bank account.
Tuesday	I feel sad ☹ Note: I do not feel like going out today. I do not want to work. I do not even want to cook meals. I do not want to eat. I just want to sleep and watch TV all day. I also so not want to shower or shave.
Wednesday	I feel angry. Note: I shouted at a waitress today because it took her more than 30 minutes to deliver my order. I also engaged in a heated argument with another driver while on my way to work.
Thursday	I feel happy ☺ I feel so good. I feel like starting a business. I also feel like starting my own band.

Friday	I feel happy ☺ I feel good and I want to book plane tickets and travel around the world next week. I do not want to sleep. I feel like I am bouncing with energy.
Saturday	I feel angry. My boss is so inconsiderate and I cannot focus on my work. I am having a hard time doing this task. I am going to call in sick tomorrow.
Sunday	I was sad this morning, but I feel happy now. My creative ideas are flowing. It is a Sunday, but I feel like working. I want to go to the office and do a special project.

2. Keep an eye on warning signs.

It is important to identify the warning signs of an incoming depressive or manic episode. Here are some of the warning signs that you may have a depressive episode:

- You do not cook meals anymore.
- You crave chocolate.
- People bother and irritate you.
- You are having severe headaches.
- You need more sleep.
- You will feel tired all the time.

Here are the warning signs that you have an incoming manic episode:

- You can't concentrate.

- You read multiple books at once.

- You are hungry all the time.

- You are crabby all the time.

- You need to move around or exercise because you have a lot of energy.

- You are talking a lot faster than usual.

3. Create a wellness checklist.

A wellness checklist is a list of all the activities and tasks that you need to do to cope with your mental disease. Coping techniques may vary so you have to create a checklist that will work for you. But, here's a list of tasks that you can use for your wellness checklist:

- Get 8 hours of sleep.

- Talk to a helpful and supportive person.

- Monitor your mood by keeping a mood journal.

- Attend a bipolar support group meeting.

- Exercise for at least thirty minutes daily.

- Ask for help from loved ones.

- Increase your exposure to light.
- Avoid alcoholic beverages.
- Avoid exposure to light.
- Do fun things.

Of course, you can write as many items as you like.

4. Avoid triggers.

You have to avoid situations that will trigger your bipolar symptoms. Here are some of the triggers of bipolar symptoms:

- Financial Difficulties
- Stress
- Seasonal Changes
- Lack of Sleep
- Problems at work
- Divorce or heartbreak
- Lack of Sleep

Try your best to avoid these triggers. Of course, if you cannot avoid it, find a way to deal with it in a healthy way.

5. Create an Emergency List.

Your emergency list should include:

- A list of all your emergency contacts such as your doctor, close family members, or therapist
- Information about your other health problems
- A list of all your medicines
- All the symptoms of your disorder
- Your treatment preferences

Give this list to your loved ones. They may need this in case you have a severe case of depression or mania.

6. Do not carry money when you are having a manic episode.

When you are having a manic episode, you are most likely to spend a lot of money. To avoid facing financial problems later on, avoid carrying money and do not bring your credit card. This will save you from making impulsive purchases.

7. Learn something new.

Channel all your energy into productive activities like learning a new language.

8. Stretch.

Do not sit at your desk for hours. Take time to get up and stretch.

9. Accept your sickness.

The only way to deal with your illness is to accept it. There is a social stigma associated with mental illness, so you may have a hard time accepting that you have this condition. Do not judge yourself. Accept your sickness and deal with it head on.

10. Have an open discussion with your doctor.

If you are uncomfortable with some of the treatment options, you have to speak out. Tell your doctor about the side effects of your medicines. Be honest. Your doctor cannot help you if you are lying about your symptoms and progress.

11. Pray.

If you believe in a higher power, take time to pray. Prayer will help you feel grounded. It will also give you a strong sense of hope.

12. Take your medicine.

Do not skip your medicine. If your body is not reacting well to the medication, let your doctor know. But, in the meantime, follow your doctor's instructions. Do not alter or skip your medication just because there are side effects.

13. Practice self love.

Do not judge yourself or berate yourself. You need love, support, and compassion. So, love yourself. Respect yourself. Be compassionate with yourself.

Rest when you feel tired. Eat when you are hungry. It is also important to maintain proper hygiene. This will help increase your confidence.

Conclusion

Thank you again for downloading this book!

I hope this book was able to help you learn more about bipolar disorder!

The next step is to put this information to use, and begin treating your bipolar disorder!

Finally, if you enjoyed this book, please take the time to share your thoughts and post a review on Amazon. It'd be greatly appreciated!

Thank you and good luck!

www.ingramcontent.com/pod-product-compliance
Lightning Source LLC
LaVergne TN
LVHW021743060526
838200LV00052B/3445